DEPENDENCY-ORIENTED THINKING

Governance And Management

I0476010

Ganesh Prasad

Dependency-Oriented Thinking
Volume 2 – Governance and Management

(Control Systems Made Simple)

Version 1.0, December 2013

Published by C4Media, publisher of InfoQ.com.

Cover illustration: Cutting the Gordian knot, re-imagined. The scales of justice refer to governance, the sword refers to execution or management, and the knot that is to be sliced is symbolic of dependencies.

Production Editor: Ana Ciobotaru
Copy Editor: Lawrence Nyveen
Cover and Interior Design: Dragos Balasoiu
Library of Congress Cataloguing-in-Publication Data:
ISBN: 978-1-329-83944-1
Printed in the United States of America
First Printing, 2014

Acknowledgements

Thanks to WSO2 for the original impetus to describe SOA governance. While there has been significant divergence from the original brief, the exercise was useful in challenging and clarifying concepts.

Also read the companion document to this one:

Dependency-Oriented Thinking: Volume 1 – Analysis and Design

(Service-Oriented Architecture Made Simple)

"That's not SOA Governance. This is SOA Governance!"
(With apologies to "Crocodile" Dundee)

Contents

PART ONE

Why the Industry Is Doing SOA Governance All Wrong

Timidity in Asserting the All-Encompassing Scope of SOA[1]

"SOA governance" does not mean the governance of SOA, any more than "scientific thinking" means "thinking about science".

We know of course that "scientific thinking" means a different way of thinking about *everything*, i.e. adopting a rigorous, analytical, evidence-based approach to understanding every aspect of the universe without exception. Scientific thinking, after all, is about applying science to thinking, not the other way around.

In exactly analogous fashion, SOA governance is about applying *SOA thinking* to governance, not about applying governance to SOA. We've been misled all along!

But then, how does one learn to "think SOA" and then apply that thinking to governance?

We must first acknowledge that SOA itself is not a set of technology products or even an approach to deploying technology components. It is an *organising principle* that impacts every aspect of the enterprise. The word "technology" refers to the *implementation of business logic*[2] and most SOA-governance activities in organisations that would say they do SOA relate to implementation-related activities such as setting development and environment standards, reviewing the design of SOAP-based Web services and business-process management (BPM), controlling versions of services, establishing policies around the use of an enterprise service bus (ESB), using a registry/repository to centralise information about services, etc. All of these are in fact routine *management* activities, with a narrow focus on technology to boot. These cannot be called SOA governance at all!

We will define SOA governance in the next section, but for now, let's start with our definition of SOA itself: *the science of analysing and managing dependencies between systems*. Systems need not be *computer* systems, and neither are dependencies restricted to technology. Dependencies exist at

---

1 Service-oriented architecture.
2 "Technology" may conjure up visions of advanced computer systems, but even a manual ledger used to record transactions is technology. Indeed, it would seem like advanced technology to a race without paper!

any level of business, human relations, *or* technology.[3] The phrase "managing dependencies" as used above is shorthand for *"eliminating needless dependencies and formalising legitimate dependencies into readily understood contracts"*.

The companion document[4] to this one contains an example of an enterprise content-management system that shows how a solution design that is tightly coupled at the data layer can completely negate the benefits of expensively procured SOA technology (e.g. ESBs, registries, etc.) Such situations are unfortunately quite common because practitioners often take a technology-only approach to SOA and do not see the dependencies that exist between systems at different levels. The fault lies not with SOA itself but in our misunderstanding of SOA as being limited to technology. We need to start seeing SOA as a way of thinking about *dependencies*, not just within the technology realm or even at the level of data, but *across the board*. Unless we adopt dependency-oriented thinking, the returns on our SOA investments will remain anaemic.[5]

It would seem that industry analysts and prominent vendors have knowingly or otherwise misled us for over a decade with the conceptual model illustrated below [Fig. 1], and this view has stood in the way of our ability to realise the full benefit of SOA. Every expert unfailingly issues the standard disclaimer that SOA is not about technology, but the opposite message gets dog-whistled through the emphasis on products to manage Web services, and ultimately prevails. In our companion document, we explain why this happens.

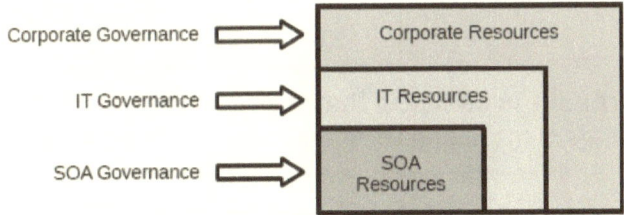

Fig. 1 – The limited (and limiting) view of SOA Governance as a subset of IT Governance (itself a subset of Corporate Governance) – a view endorsed by industry thought leaders such as the Burton Group[6] and IBM[7].

---

3 The companion document Dependency-Oriented Thinking Volume 1 provides numerous case studies to emphasise the importance of dependencies.
4 *Dependency-Oriented Thinking: Volume 1 – Analysis and Design*
5 In retrospect, DOT (dependency-oriented thinking) may have been a better term than SOA.

To repeat, SOA is *not* a subset of IT. It is a generic organising principle with universal applicability. The benefits of SOA thinking when applied more broadly are:

An **improvement in business agility** because of minimal dependencies between systems and consequently minimal friction that can impede change.

Sustainably **lower operating costs** for the same reasons.

A significant **reduction in operational risk** because of better-understood dependencies and fewer surprises.

Clearly, we have lost out on some major benefits by defining SOA as narrowly as we have.

Confusion Between Governance and Management

"Governance" is an overused (and abused) term. One of the unfortunate side effects of the collapse of corporations like Enron and WorldCom in 2001-2002 was the sudden popularity of the term "governance" in popular discourse. The word "governance" has acquired such a cachet today that it often tends to be used just for effect, even when what is meant is just plain old "management". So let's set these terms apart right away.

**Governance is ensuring that the right things are done.
Management is ensuring that things are done right.**

In spirit, governance is about the ends, or the "what"; management is about the means, or the "how". This is a fundamental distinction that is key to correctly implementing what we recommend in this document, and it is worth spending some effort to understand this thoroughly.

An analogy with the functions of a company's board of directors and its executive management will make the distinction between corporate governance and corporate management more concrete. A decision on whether the company should enter a new market is a decision for the board, because it pertains to the fundamentals of what the company wants to be and whether or not the move is in the best interests of its shareholders. In other words, this is about doing the right thing (i.e. governance).

Once the decision is taken to enter a new market, executive management is responsible for retooling the resources of the company to enable it to compete effectively in that market. This is about doing things right (i.e. management).

Governance and management decisions apply at lower levels of the organisation as well.

Projects often have steering committees as well as working groups. Steering committees are comprised of key stakeholders and they tend to make *governance* (i.e. "what") decisions: objectives, scope, success criteria, etc. They also monitor adherence to these parameters. Working groups are teams of hands-on people assigned to the project. They make the day-to-day *management* (i.e. "how") decisions that will enable them to solve routine problems and achieve the objectives that have been set by the steering committee. The steering committee is only concerned with the ends and not the means. The working group is responsible for the means.

In general, one can tell whether a given decision is about governance or about management by thinking about how those decisions could be judged in hindsight. If the verdict is likely to be "right" or "wrong", then it's a governance decision. If the assessment is likely to be one of a spectrum (e.g. "excellent", "good", "fair", or "poor"), then it's a management decision.

Obesity of the Governance Function

Organisations that have embraced the requirement for "SOA Governance" generally have committees, processes, and tools to bring discipline to the way services are designed, built, deployed, and managed. After all, this is how the governance of SOA is commonly interpreted. Some organisations have an integration centre of competence that is tasked with defining standards and controlling the introduction of new services into the ecosystem.

While these are sensible measures, they impose a rather high overhead especially given their limited technology-only focus. A centralised approving authority is an overworked bottleneck, and so agility and operational cost are the first casualties. Many organisations consequently see very modest improvements in their operational cost and efficiency as a result of moving to SOA. The economies and dis-economies largely neutralise each other, and the heavyweight governance processes shoulder a large portion of the blame.

If projects in your organisation are constantly trying to find short cuts around a centralised authority and a large part of this latter group's efforts aim at reigning in such rogue projects, it could be a sign that the organisation is chafing under heavyweight governance.

PART
TWO

Elements of a Common-Sense Approach

Back to First Principles and the Notion of "Dependencies"

The four most important principles of SOA are dependencies, dependencies, dependencies, and dependencies.[1] We're not being entirely flippant in saying this, because there are four distinct layers in an organisation where dependencies need to be managed. These layers, as we will explain shortly with the help of a formal framework, are business, applications, information (data), and technology.[2]

We believe that for an organisation to be effective in achieving its goals, an acceptance of this dependency-based view of SOA is essential [Fig. 2]. Any discussion of SOA governance and SOA management has to start from this basis.

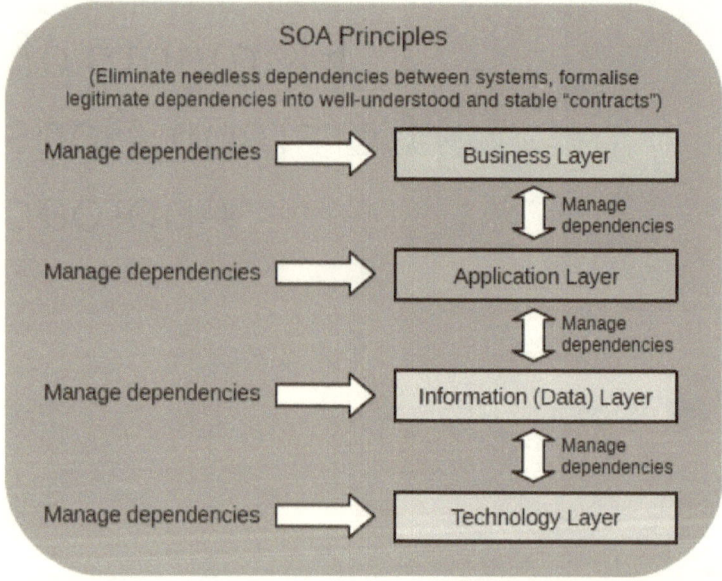

Fig. 2 – The True Scope and Concerns of SOA

- More than just a few Web Services managed by a section of IT!

Since SOA is all about the management of dependencies, SOA governance should be seen as deciding *what* dependencies are legitimate and SOA management as deciding *how* to manage dependencies. Both these

---

1   To paraphrase the three rules of real estate: "location, location, location".
2   This is commonly referred to as the BAIT model.

aspects are important, so even though SOA governance seems to have all the mind-share, this document will talk about SOA management[3] with equal emphasis. Ironically, traditional approaches to SOA governance are usually about SOA management (i.e. the "how").

So here are our simple and readily understandable definitions:

SOA governance is determining *what* dependencies are legitimate at every layer of the organisation and identifying *what* existing dependencies fall outside this set.

SOA management deals with *how* to remediate illegitimate dependencies at every layer of the organisation, *how* to formally document and communicate legitimate dependencies, and *how* to prevent recurring violations.

We will break these down into specific tasks in Part III, but for now, the following high-level illustration [Fig. 3] will summarise how we arrive at these definitions.

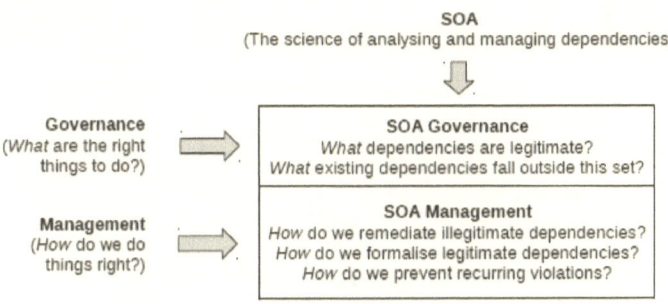

Fig. 3 – SOA Governance and SOA Management at a glance

This is the core philosophy behind our approach to SOA governance and SOA management in this document. Let us see how we can approach the analysis of dependencies in a systematic way. This is what SOA governance and SOA management are really about.

---

3 In the literature, we often come across the term "service management". This term derives from the view of SOA as a subset of IT rather than as a set of organising principles for the entire enterprise. Our term "SOA management" is more comprehensive.

An Architectural Framework to Analyse Dependencies

We need a framework to analyse dependencies before we determine how to govern and manage them. Rather than reinvent the wheel, let's look at some existing and well-understood models to see if they suit our requirements. The following sections on BAIT are paraphrased for convenience from our companion document, *Dependency-Oriented Thinking: Volume 1 – Analysis and Design.*

Introducing the BAIT Model

We briefly saw what the four layers of the BAIT model looked like. BAIT is a popular architectural framework that decomposes an organisation into four layers: business, applications, information (data), and technology. The four layers deal with the following:

- Business layer – business entities

- Application layer – applications and systems

- Information (data) layer – domain data models

- Technology layer – technology standards, hardware, and software

BAIT has the right idea about layers, but it is traditionally focused on identifying the *entities* that exist at each layer and the *relationships* between those entities. It does not inherently emphasise *dependencies*, even when dealing with relationships. When we adopt the BAIT model to aid us in SOA, we have to adapt it to focus on dependencies.

BAIT As a Model of Dependency Types

The most basic perspective comes from asking what *type* of dependency each layer is responsible for, and this leads to what we will call the "Four I" model shown below [Fig. 4].

Business Layer	Business "Intent"
Application Layer	Internal Cohesion
Information Layer	Interfaces and Integration
Technology Layer	Implementation

Fig. 4 – The "Four I" Model of SOA

From this viewpoint, we could postulate that each layer covers one of four I's, referring respectively to the:

- **Intent**, i.e. dependencies arising as a natural consequence of what the business wants to do.

- **Internal cohesion**, i.e. dependencies that dictate how related units of functionality coalesce into discrete logical components.

- **Interfaces/integration**, i.e. dependencies *between* such logical components (to be kept to the minimum).

- **Implementation**, i.e. dependencies arising (or more importantly, *not* arising!) from how logical components are physically implemented.

BAIT As a Model of Operations

Another way of looking at the BAIT model [Fig. 5] is how it relates to the core notion of operations (i.e. process steps), which are the building blocks of SOA.

Business Layer	Determine Operations
Application Layer	Group Operations
Information Layer	Expose Operations
Technology Layer	Execute and Coordinate Operations

Fig. 5 – SOA as "Operation-Oriented Architecture"

In this view, each layer of the BAIT model performs a different function with respect to operations. The **business** layer is where operations are first identified or determined, based on what the business wants to do and the high-level processes that are required to support those goals. The business layer therefore also determines the *dynamic* grouping of operations (process steps) into processes as a natural consequence of its analysis.

The **application** layer determines the *static* grouping of operations into (what else?) applications, based on factors that cause them to belong together. We will see two types of applications that differ only in the criteria used for such grouping.

The **information** layer determines the most stable (i.e. robust in the face of change) way to expose operations to other systems, by identifying the simplest interface data model that defines the essence of the operation and abstracts the many flavours or variants it may need to support. A stable interface also reduces the need for frequent versioning.

The **technology** layer groups operations into deployment bundles and has tooling to host these bundles of operations and execute the business logic inside each. At this layer, there are also description bundles that show other systems how to invoke operations. There is also tooling for processes that can coordinate operations exposed in this way. All of these are done in accordance with well-understood and accepted standards.[4]

We will use elements of both the above views of BAIT in our approach.

TOGAF[5] Artefacts As Dependency Relationships

The TOGAF framework of enterprise architecture builds on the BAIT model and describes generic entities in each layer along with their inter-relationships. This is extremely valuable to us when embarking on SOA governance and SOA management because the hard work of understanding the components of an organisation and how they fit together has already been done.

However, just like with BAIT itself, TOGAF as it stands is not a perfect framework that can be used without adaptation to our treatment of SOA governance and SOA management. It does not inherently support the *dependency-oriented* organisational transformation that we would like to model and plan for. SOA is a single isolated chapter in The Open Group's 780-page *TOGAF Version 9* book, which betrays a traditionalist view of SOA as a subset of IT rather than as the science of analysing and managing

---

4 Ideally, no new dependencies are introduced in the course of implementation.
5 The Open Group Architecture Framework: http://www.opengroup.org/togaf/

dependencies across the board. However, nothing prevents us from using a dependency lens to view the detailed set of entity relationships identified by TOGAF and derive a more applicable model for our requirements. We'll show how to do that in Part III of this document.

TOGAF defines some core concepts at the four layers and lists out some important and standardised documents ("viewpoints" in the TOGAF terminology) that provide useful information about these concepts and their interactions. TOGAF uses the term "catalog" to refer to any list. Similarly, it uses the term "matrix" for tables that show the relationship between exactly two concepts, and "diagram" for any depiction of how more than two concepts are related [Fig. 6].

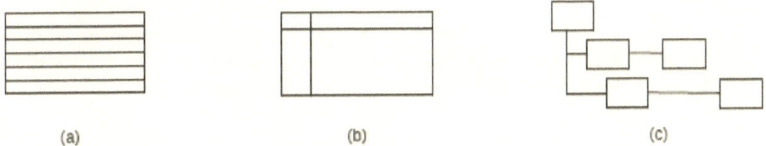

(a)   (b)   (c)

Fig. 6 – (a) a TOGAF "catalog", or list of entities; (b) a TOGAF "matrix", or table of two-entity relationships; (c) a TOGAF "diagram", or a depiction of multi-entity relationships.

If we interpret relationships as dependencies, matrices become two-entity dependencies and diagrams become multi-entity dependencies. The set of TOGAF-defined matrices and diagrams at each of the four BAIT layers then gives us a ready-made checklist of the dependencies we need to be mindful of within those layers as well as between layers.

We consciously adapt TOGAF's set of artefacts to align them with a SOA view of the enterprise because TOGAF is not inherently dependency-oriented. In other words, the entity dependencies we study will correspond to our SOA version of the BAIT model [Fig. 7] rather than the traditional one.

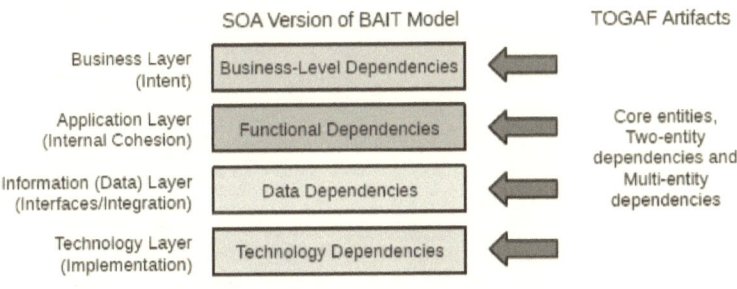

Fig. 7 – TOGAF artifacts classified by BAIT level

We can now begin to see why the traditional view of SOA governance is so limited [Fig. 8].

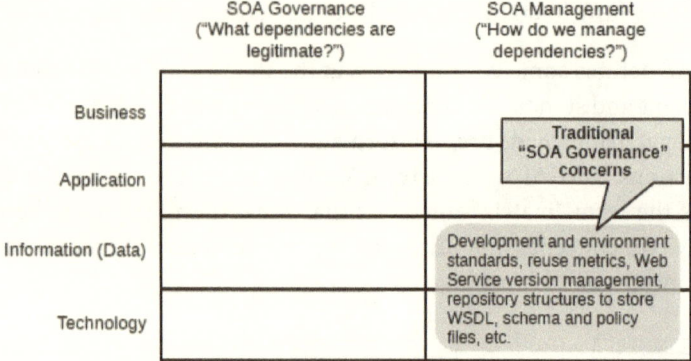

Fig. 8 – Traditional "SOA Governance" concerns are more correctly SOA Management, and a subset at that. Little effort is focused on the governance question, "What dependencies are legitimate?"

Clearly, our entire approach needs nothing less than an overhaul. It's time to look at how SOA governance and SOA management should in fact be done.

PART
THREE

A Practical Guide to Governing and Managing Dependencies

In the previous two parts of this document, we critiqued the industry's approach to SOA governance and suggested how we could do it better by considering the elements of a more rational approach based on the analysis of dependencies.

In this part of the document, we will show how to put these elements together into a lightweight method. We'll recommend some key roles and bodies that will be responsible for the functions of SOA governance and SOA management, the minimal set of processes they need to carry out, and a manageable set of checklists that they should use for these purposes.

Agencies and Vehicles

Key Roles

We believe that the primary agency to apply dependency-oriented thinking at every level of an organisation is the enterprise-architecture function. In organisations with an enterprise-architecture group, there are usually architects with specialised skills who are tasked with defining the business architecture, application architecture, data architecture, and technology architecture, so the BAIT model is already an operational tool. These specialised architects are the people who need to spearhead a new way of approaching SOA governance and SOA management.

The role of enterprise architecture under this model is to analyse the four layers of the organisation *specifically from a dependency focus*, first to determine the "what" (the legitimate dependencies that should exist at each level as well as the unnecessary ones that do currently exist) and then to guide the "how" (the programs of work required to align the organisation to the set of legitimate dependencies that were identified).

One of the suggestions we have for the enterprise-architecture function to assist them in transitioning to this worldview is to include professionals from certain other disciplines, even if on a part-time basis. Project managers, risk managers, and contract lawyers are all used to looking for dependencies in their own areas, and they can inject some of the fresh blood that the traditional enterprise-architecture group needs to make them effective in a SOA sense.

In organisations with a reasonably effective architecture function, here's how business intent is transformed into working systems today [Fig. 9].

Fig. 9 – Key roles and their traditional concerns

Here's the subtle but important change we would like to see [Fig. 10]:

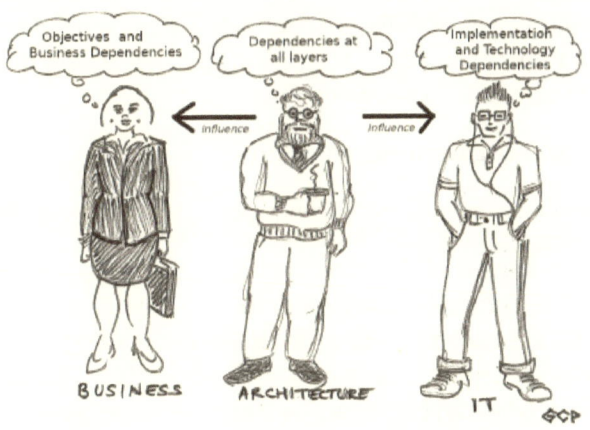

Fig. 10 – Key roles and their recommended concerns

It's not as if architects don't already think about dependencies. It's just that dependencies need to be promoted to be a primary, top-of-mind item in all discussions and decisions, especially where the business and IT are involved. Every individual who is part of the decision chain from business objective to implementation, no matter what their level, needs to be sensitised to the importance of dependencies. That's what it means to inculcate SOA thinking within an organisation, and architects need to don the mantle of evangelists to spread this philosophy.

The perspectives of project managers, risk managers, and contract lawyers could be very useful additions to their skill set, since these give them fresh pairs of eyes with which to recognise the diverse set of dependencies impacting the enterprise.

SOA governance and SOA management become far easier to execute when the organisational culture understands the importance of dependencies.

Key Bodies

While the enterprise-architecture function is key to our recommended approach, SOA governance and SOA management require the active participation of many different roles and functions to be effective. The business and IT are crucial stakeholders, as we saw. It is essential to involve multiple roles in the SOA governance and SOA management functions, and this calls for new organisational structures. We are all too aware of the reputation of committees as inefficient bureaucracies,[1] but the multidisciplinary nature of the tasks at hand, together with the fact that these are on-going responsibilities, dictate the need for one or more standing bodies rather than *ad hoc* teams. Broadly, two groups of people are required to carry out the required functions:

- a dependency governance committee

- a dependency management committee

Now, this is a functional classification, and these two logical groups could be realised as several physical committees, e.g. one or more at each level of the BAIT model plus one at the enterprise level. Some committees could also take responsibility for more than one BAIT layer, as long as they are clear which layer they are dealing with at any given time.

The decision on how many physical committees to have is entirely up to the organisation in question, but we would strongly recommend against combining governance and management functions within any single committee. That would defeat one of our primary goals, which is to perform both functions effectively and without confusion.

Additionally, although it's the committees' *functions* that are important and not their names, we would recommend that the term "dependency" be explicitly used in their names in order to inculcate a dependency focus

---

1 Two of our personal favourites are "A camel is a horse designed by a committee," and "A committee is a group of people who individually can do nothing, but who get together to decide that nothing can be done."

within every person in the organisation. We've lost a decade's worth of benefits thanks to poor naming ("service-oriented" as opposed to "dependency-oriented"), so let's call a spade a spade this time, however corny it may sound. A committee should either be a dependency governance committee or a dependency-management committee, with prefixes as appropriate to the BAIT level and/or business unit.

In a nutshell,

The **dependency governance committee** is responsible for defining which of the dependencies at the level they are responsible for are legitimate and which are not. They are also responsible for prioritising the programs of work to remediate dependencies.

The **dependency-management committee** is responsible for pricing, planning, and initiating the programs of work that will bring and keep the organisation in line with the model validated by the dependency governance committee and according to the priority decided by that committee.

The **dependency governance committee** should have a fair representation of enterprise architects, with specialists in each of the BAIT layers. At least some of the members of the dependency governance committee should have a background in one of the non-IT professions listed earlier,[2] because these professionals are trained to look for dependencies. Depending on the layer of the BAIT model for which the committee is responsible, there should be representation from senior executives, business managers, functional heads, and technology specialists. This may mean separate committees or a single committee with some fixed members and a number of others who attend only the sessions that are relevant to them.

Importantly, the dependency governance committee must have authority and access to funding to be able to approve programs of work, otherwise the organisation will be unable to remediate the dependencies identified as invalid. Our companion document on analysis and design has a number of real-life case studies to hammer home the idea that attention to dependencies saves *real money*. Business-unit heads should therefore not be churlish about funding dependency-remediation tasks, and their representation on governance committees serves more than just a decorative function!

---

2 Project managers, risk managers, and contract lawyers.

The **dependency-management committee** should comprise people skilled in costing and planning, typically project managers and functional heads. They may need representation from enterprise architecture to keep them focused on the dependency aspect while they attend to their more familiar roles of pricing and planning programs of work. Again, there will be a need to have different people engaged for different layers of the BAIT model, so there could be considerable variety in the structure and/or composition of the committee(s).

How Many Committees?

The dependency-governance and management functions can be performed by just two committees in a small organisation, since they can do justice to the complexity of the entire organisation themselves. As organisations become larger, the committees will need to become more specialised, as the following examples illustrate [Fig. 11 to 13].

Dependency Governance Committee	Dependency Management Committee

Fig. 11 – Committees for a small organisation

Enterprise Dependency Governance Committee	Enterprise Dependency Management Committee
Business Dependency Governance Committee	Business Dependency Management Committee
Application & Information Dependency Governance Committee	Application & Information Dependency Management Committee
Technology Dependency Governance Committee	Technology Dependency Management Committee

Fig. 12 – Committees for a medium-sized organisation

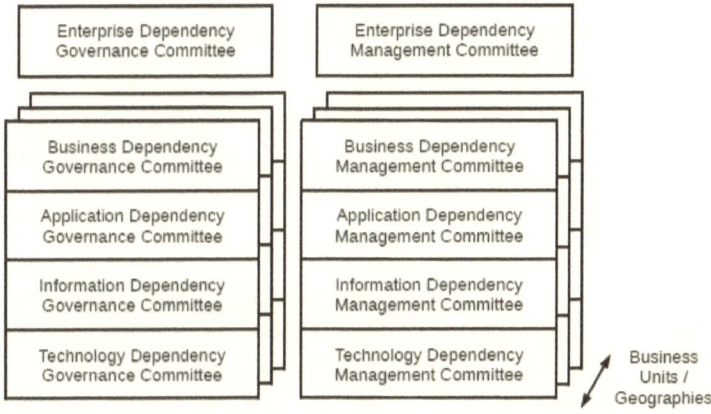

Fig. 13 – Committees for a large organisation

If this set of committees is beginning to look too bloated, our audacious claim is that these are the *only* governance and management structures that an organisation will ever need, so this could in fact represent a drastic *simplification* to the plethora of management bodies that currently exist in a given organisation.

Let's look at a few special cases to support this claim.

Security dependencies: Security is an important aspect of business operations, and information security traditionally tends to be treated as an IT concern. However, security concerns are relevant at different levels of the BAIT model. Perimeter security, for example, may be relevant only at the level of technology, since it is completely opaque to higher layers. Data-leakage protection applies at all levels from the business layer down, since it is impacted by business processes, application design, data interchange, and technology-related aspects like USB-device control and disk encryption. PCI-DSS[3] compliance requirements may or may not impact business processes but will certainly impact application design, data storage, and encryption/tokenisation technology. The dependency-governance and management committees at these various levels will address and manage the security concerns listed above, as well as any others that arise from time to time.

---

3 Payment-Card Industry Data Security Standard

Non-technology domains that are not line-of-business, such as human resources, accounting, finance, or legal, also fit into this dependency-oriented model.

Human-resources dependencies: Clearly, an organisation that employs many more contractors than permanent employees has a very different dependency profile than one with the opposite composition. The contractor-based organisation can downsize more readily in an economic downturn and re-hire when required, but it has a more tenuous hold on IP due to the less sticky nature of employee knowledge. The contractor-based organisation will have to invest more heavily into knowledge-management systems to mitigate against their risk of losing critical business and operations knowledge. The organisation with a higher proportion of permanent employees will have to be more cautious about hiring in an economic upturn because of their larger financial exposure arising from retrenchment benefits they may have to pay out when downsizing. A business dependency governance committee and business dependency-management committee focused on the HR business unit will be able to formalise these concerns and evolve mitigating strategies.

Finance dependencies: An organisation that is funded mainly by debt has a different dependency profile than one funded mainly by equity. A debtor and a creditor represent dependencies of different kinds, and every financial instrument that is issued or purchased imposes a different flavour of dependency on the enterprise. Even within a single organisation, the dependencies between divisions are often expressed through mechanisms such as transfer pricing. Financial controllers make decisions based on such dependencies all the time, whether or not they use the word "dependency". Regardless, the business dependency-governance and management committees for the finance business unit will standardise these functions in a consistent corporate style.

IT dependencies: In a new twist on the old "SOA is technology" mindset, it may be argued that the bulk of a modern enterprise's business logic tends to be coded into software-based systems with very little residual manual processing, so "it's all IT anyway." Let us refute this argument with a simple analogy. Just because all legal documents in a country are in the English language does not imply that a mastery of English is all that is required to understand or to draft legal documents. One needs to understand law. In similar fashion, even if every piece of business logic in an organisation is implemented within a technology platform, it is not sufficient to understand how to govern and manage technology. The business principles behind every aspect of the organisation's functioning need to be understood, and the analysis of dependencies is a crucial tool to achieve this understanding.

In short, these varied examples support our claim that SOA, being all about dependencies, is not about technology but is an organising principle for the enterprise and lends itself to a simple and consistent form of governance and management. Form follows function, and the structure of the required governance and management committees follows the discipline of dependency-oriented thinking.

Functions and Processes

Broadly speaking, the processes required for SOA governance and SOA management are either *one-time* or *recurring*.

To keep an otherwise dry topic light and readable, we will illustrate what occurs during each of these processes [Fig. 14] through imaginary conversations between various parties. The players in all these scenarios are the following:

G – Dependency-governance committee

M – Dependency-management committee

B – Any business unit

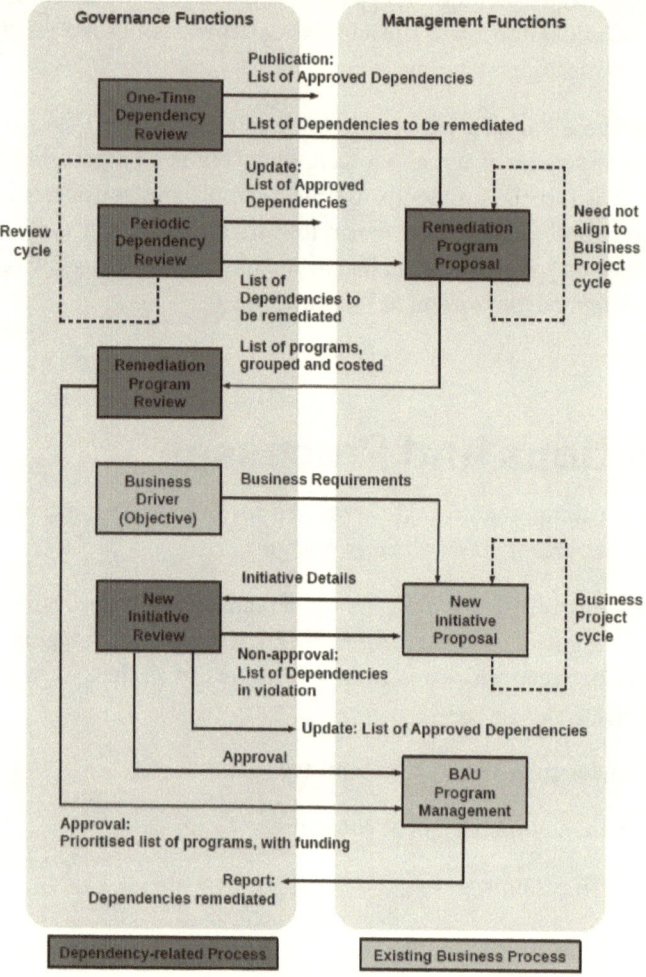

Fig. 14 – Dependency Governance and Management Processes

One-Time Processes

When an organisation embarks on SOA governance and management the way this document recommends, there will be a one-time activity (which could of course be broken up into phases for manageability) on the part of the dependency governance committee to do two things:

Agree on the set of approved dependencies at each level of the organisation as suggested by the BAIT model.

Identify the dependencies that actually exist, specifically the ones that fall outside the set of approved dependencies above.

The latter list (the set of actual dependencies that are not approved) is the input provided to the dependency-management committee to plan a program of work to remediate.

Initial Dependency Review

Scenario:

G: "We've done a review and decided that the only legitimate dependencies are these. There are many actual dependencies we've found in our systems that are not in this approved set. They need to be eliminated."

M: "OK, we'll come back with a proposal for a program of work to remediate them."

Recurring Processes

There are recurring processes within both the governance and management functions.

Recurring *governance* processes are reviews to revalidate the set of legitimate dependencies at any level and to identify afresh the set of existing dependencies that fall outside of this approved set. The latter set (which is expected to shrink with each iteration) is then an input to management committees to initiate programs of work to remediate. Prioritisation and approval of these proposed programs of work is also a governance function.

Periodic Dependency Review

Scenario 1:

G: "Given the changing nature of our business since the last review, some new dependencies are now deemed legitimate and some old ones no longer are."

M: "OK, we'll make a note of the new set of approved dependencies and come back to you with a proposal for a program of work to eliminate the ones that are no longer approved."

Scenario 2:

G: "Some new dependencies that are not in the approved list seem to have snuck into our systems since our last review. These need to be eliminated ASAP."

M: "We don't understand how that could have happened. We'll come back to you with a proposal for a program of work to remediate them."

Remediation-Program Review

M: "We've put together a proposal for a set of programs that will remediate the unapproved dependencies that you identified. We've worked out the costs and benefits of each of them. Please tell us how you would like to prioritise them for execution, and please approve funding for the ones you want done in the current period."

G: "We think you should initiate the following subset of programs in the current reporting period and defer the remaining for a future period. The funding for the programs in the current period is hereby approved."

M: "We'll initiate these programs right away."

Recurring *management* processes are intended to identify programs of work to remediate the invalid dependencies identified by the governance committee(s) and to manage these programs once approved by them.

Remediation-Program Proposal

Scenario 1:

M (internal conversation): "Given the set of existing dependencies that were identified by the dependency governance committee as not being on the approved list, let's work out the costs and benefits of eliminating them, and group these tasks into cohesive programs of work for them to prioritise and approve."

Business-As-Usual Program Management

Once a dependency remediation program is approved, it is managed in exactly identical fashion to regular business projects. These are not to be treated as projects of secondary importance or nice-to-haves because of a mistaken characterisation of SOA as technology. On the contrary, the involvement of business and technology representatives and proper positioning of the benefits of these initiatives by enterprise architecture should ensure that they are taken equally seriously as programs initiated by the business. After all, unfixed dependencies mean significant amounts of real money, as we have seen earlier.

The business initiatives detailed in the next section also feed into business-as-usual (BAU) program management alongside dependency remediation programs.

The standard discipline of conducting post-implementation reviews (PIRs) to evaluate the success of a program should be conducted for dependency remediation initiatives as well. Granted, the benefits are not always immediate but recurring, but it should be possible to assess if the dependencies slated for elimination were in fact removed, and a fresh assessment of the costs and benefits of the initiative should be conducted to report back to the dependency governance committee.

New-Initiative Appraisal

An event that could trigger a fresh governance activity is when there is a business driver (objective) necessitating a program of work, the proposal is put forward, and the governance committee evaluates if this introduces any fresh dependencies that are not on the approved list. (Of course, any additional dependencies may be justified, in which case the approved list is updated, or may even make some existing dependencies unnecessary, which again results in updates to the approved list.) The proposal may need to be amended to avoid introducing dependencies that are not approved.

A new initiative could be on the business side – e.g. entering a new market, introducing a new product, acquiring a company, outsourcing or re-insourcing a business function, changing a business process, signing up a new partnership, etc.

The initiative could also be on the technology side – e.g. buying and installing a new product system, developing a new system in-house, outsourcing or re-insourcing a technology function, changing the technology implementation of a function or process, decommissioning a system or application, undertaking a turnkey project, etc.

All of these changes have dependency implications that require review before the initiatives concerned can be approved. A large part of the technical and business debt that is incurred by organisations is due to a failure to assess new initiatives for their dependency implications.

The following process is meant to plug that loophole.

Scenario 1:

B: "Here's our proposal for a new project."

G: "It appears that your project is about to eliminate some dependencies. That's good. Project approved."

B: "Thanks. We'll initiate the project."

M: "We'll make a note that the set of approved (and existing) dependencies will shrink after this project."

Scenario 2:

B: "Here's our proposal for a new project."

G: "Your project introduces a new set of dependencies, but they do seem to be valid, so we'll expand the set of approved dependencies. Project approved."

B: "Thanks. We'll initiate the project."

M: "We'll make a note of the expanded set of approved dependencies."

Scenario 3:

B: "Here's our proposal for a new project."

G: "Your project will introduce new dependencies that are not valid. We're afraid we can't approve it. Go back and re-think your processes and/or designs so that they stay within the set of approved dependencies."

B: "OK. We'll get back to you with a reworked proposal."

M: ("Nothing for us to do.")

Incorporating a Dependency Focus into New-Initiative Appraisal

The business case for any program of work should include its impact on dependencies (positive or negative) in addition to the standard calculations of cost-to-implement and business benefit. Dependencies carry a hidden yet heavy cost in terms of business agility, operating cost, and operational risk, so we would like to have these made explicit and brought to the notice of approving authorities. Introducing dependencies (legitimate or not) incurs cost and risk, and removing them has the opposite effect. This is where the work done by governance committees in identifying dependencies will form a useful input. A simplified form that illustrates this is shown below [Fig. 15].

New-Initiative Appraisal Form

	Cost		Business Benefit	Dependency impacts (+/-)		
Description of proposed project	CapEx	OpEx	(3 Yrs)	Business agility	Operating costs	Operational risk
		(3 Yrs)		(3 Yrs)	(3 Yrs)	assessment
Remove replication of customer	(200,000)	(25,000)	90,000	50,000	80,000	Changes from
address data by consolidating it		(25,000)	90,000	50,000	80,000	medium to low
within system X where it belongs		(25,000)	90,000	50,000	80,000	

Approved by:

Approval date:

Fig. 15 – An indicative format for a "New Initiative Appraisal Form"

The form above illustrates how hidden benefits from the removal of dependencies (or, conversely, the hidden costs of introducing fresh dependencies), once quantified, could sway the business case for a project either way. In this example, the business case for a proposed project doesn't by itself stack up because the total business benefit over a three-year ROI horizon ($270,000) is less than the cost incurred ($275,000).

However, the benefit goes up enormously once the improvements to the organisation's agility, cost, and risk profile are taken into account. A dependency focus therefore drives behaviour that is desirable over the longer term. This is the kind of change we would like to see in the way organisations evaluate programs of work. It represents a least-dependency model of doing business which keeps them lean and low-risk.

Processes in Steady State

The recurring processes around dependency review followed by remediation are expected to wind down as the culture of dependency-sensitivity begins to take hold and the number of exceptions correspondingly reduces.

In steady state [Fig. 16], the only processes that we are likely to see are new-initiative proposal, new-initiative review and BAU program management, since these processes will subsume the dependency-related activities that are the sole focus of the other processes. Periodic dependency reviews will still take place but, with any luck, no deviations will have occurred and hence no remediation programs will need to be initiated.

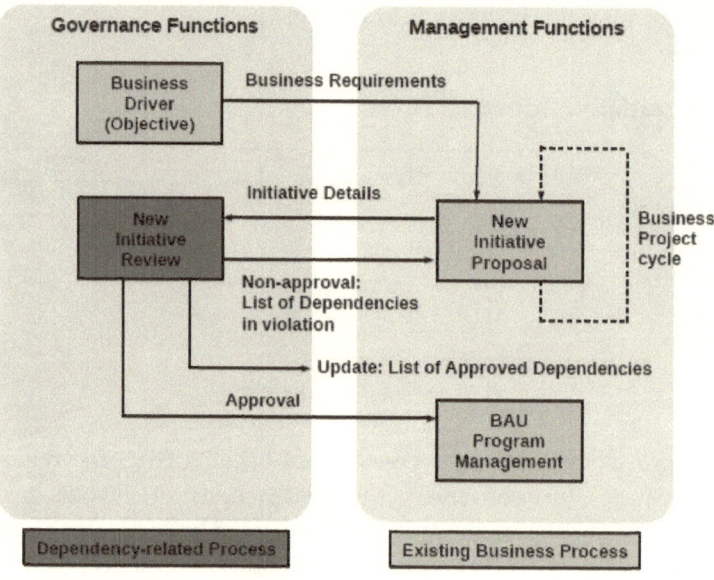

Fig. 16 – Ideal Dependency Governance and Management Processes in "Steady State"

Governance and Management Checklists

With our governance/management bodies and processes in place, it's time to look at what they will actually do. Here is a recommended approach based on a detailed analysis of organisational layers along with a sample checklist of questions for the committees to ask.

Classification of Dependencies

Consider a set of dependencies between entities within a BAIT layer (or across layers) [Fig. 17].

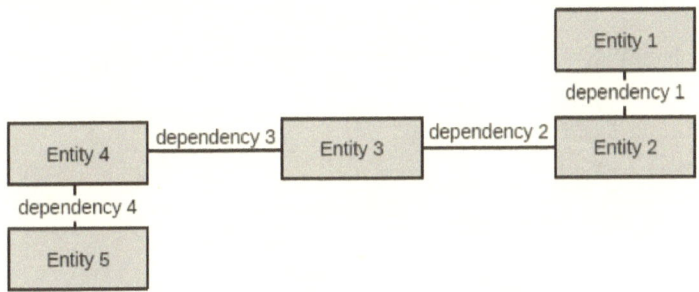

Fig. 17 – An unclassified set of dependencies

These dependencies may be further categorised into, say, two broad groups [Fig. 18] because they are themselves related in some way. A governance or management committee may then assign responsibility for these two dependency groups to two separate teams.

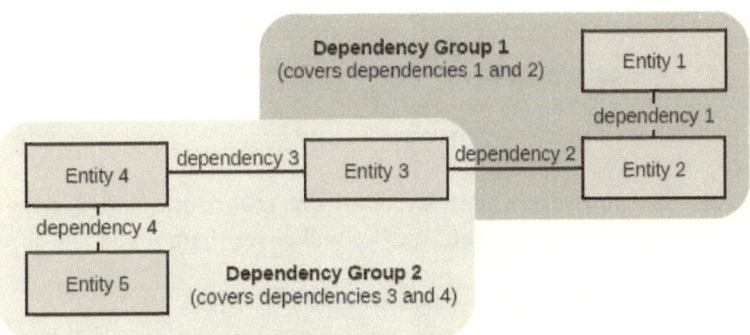

Fig. 18 – Dependency Groups containing cohesive sets of dependencies

The dependency governance committee(s) and dependency-management committee(s) may want to organise themselves into specialised teams to study and monitor smaller, cohesive sets of dependencies. We will call this intermediate level of granularity (i.e. somewhere between a single dependency and all the dependencies that may exist at a BAIT layer) a "dependency group". Although not identified in TOGAF, a dependency group helps to provide a "system" view of related dependencies.

In the following sections, we will document not just the set of dependencies suggested by TOGAF at each BAIT layer, but also our suggested classification of these dependencies into dependency groups that can be assigned to specialised teams as their responsibility.

The List of Checklists

Our checklists will be numbered according to the following scheme:

	G(overnance)	M(anagement)
Basic	G-00	M-00
E(nterprise)	EG-00	EM-00
B(usiness)	BG-00	BM-00
A(pplication)	AG-00	AM-00
I(nformation)	IG-00	IM-00
T(echnology)	TG-00	TM-00

A Basic Governance Checklist

Regardless of the level of the BAIT model at which governance will be applied, there are some standard questions that will need to be asked:

G-01	What are the core entities involved?
G-02	What are the legitimate dependencies between them?
G-03	What dependencies can we identify in the current situation that fall outside this set of legitimate dependencies?

There will of course be more specialised governance questions depending on the BAIT layer concerned, and we will cover them under the appropriate sections.

A Basic Management Checklist

In similar fashion, there are some standard management questions that need to be asked at every level of the BAIT model:

M-01	How do we express the dependencies between entities as suitable contracts?
M-02	How will we enforce contracts?
M-03	How will we monitor adherence to contracts?
M-04	How do we re-engineer our existing systems to align them with the target model?

Every BAIT layer will add its own specialised management questions to this list, and we will examine each under its corresponding section.

When an organisation's governance and management committees are staffed with appropriate experts and when they adapt to the dependency-oriented way of thinking, they will be able to formulate more relevant questions to add to these checklists.

Fundamental Enterprise Dependencies and Dependency Checklists

Before we even go into the four BAIT layers, we need to understand some fundamental dependencies at the overall organisational level as illustrated below. The reason why the enterprise has been split from even the business layer is that most organisations are highly siloed at the business-unit level (from immediately below the CEO). Hence enterprise concerns need to be addressed at a level higher than those of business units.

The dependency governance committee at this level is necessarily high-powered. It should consist of the head of architecture and the CIO engaging with the CEO and executive management. This is the only body that can authoritatively decide on the legitimate dependencies at the enterprise level.

The dependency governance committee should review these dependencies on a periodic basis, perhaps half-yearly. Any deviations in practice should be referred to a dependency-management committee, which may consist of the executive management and their direct reports. The dependency-management committee will be responsible for bringing the organisation back into alignment with the approved set of enterprise dependencies.

The four broad dependency groups at the fundamental enterprise level are as below [Fig. 19], and different skill groups may be engaged to deal with each:

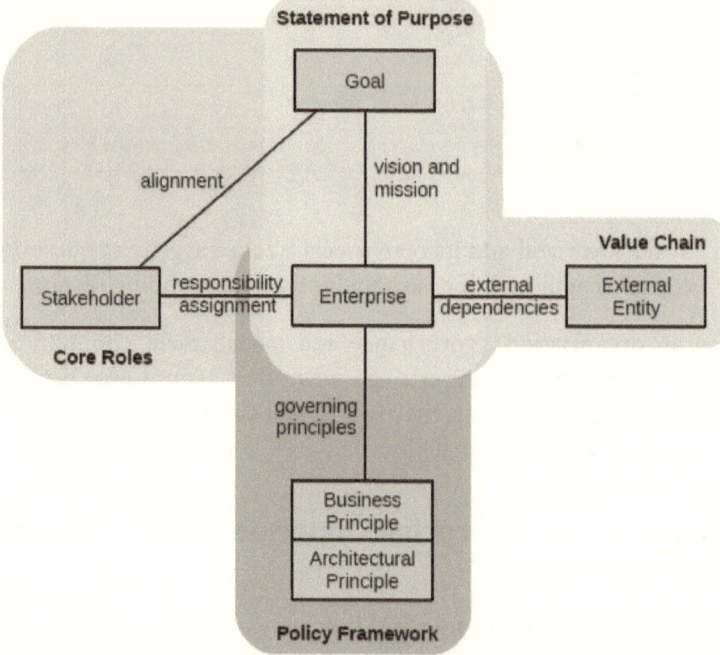

Fig. 19 – Dependencies and Dependency Groups at the Enterprise level (TOGAF)

1. The **statement of purpose** associates the enterprise with its goals through vision and mission statements. The vision is the enterprise's opinion of what its utopia would look like. The mission defines the role the enterprise asserts for itself to bring about that vision of utopia.

Sample Governance Questions:

EG-01	What is the Enterprise's concept of Utopia? (Vision statement)
EG-02	What is the Enterprise's role in bringing about that Utopia? (Mission statement)
EG-03	What is the rationale for the Mission statement?

Sample Management Questions:

EM-01	How do we communicate our concept of Utopia?
EM-02	How do we execute our self-appointed role? (The answer to this question creates the foundation of the business architecture.)

2. The **value chain** describes the dependencies between the enterprise and important external entities.

Sample Governance Questions:

EG-04	What are the dependencies that external entities have on the enterprise? (This is the reverse of the basic governance question of what dependencies the enterprise has on external entities.)
EG-05	What alternative external entities can feasibly replace our current ones without impact?
EG-06	What *abstract* external entities do we have a dependency on (e.g., the economy, the regulatory environment)?
EG-07	What external entities may also be considered partially internal (e.g., head office, subsidiaries)?
EG-08	What time-bound contractual obligations currently exist (that can be re-negotiated at an appropriate juncture)?

Sample Management Questions:

EM-03	How do we reduce the leverage that external entities have over us?
EM-04	How do we increase the leverage that we have over external entities?

3. **Core roles** describe how responsibilities are assigned to stakeholders within the enterprise, usually through a RACI/RASCI[4] model.

---

4 RASCI stands for Responsible, Accountable, Supports/Sponsors, Consulted, Informed. This is a model of responsibility assignment that usually takes the form of a matrix and visually displays the coverage of responsibilities across roles. There are many variants of this.

Sample Governance Questions:

EG-09	What gaps currently exist in the set of stakeholders in terms of responsibility assignments?
EG-10	What overlaps currently exist in the set of stakeholders in terms of responsibility assignments?
EG-11	What set of stakeholders (in terms of responsibility assignments) best covers the requirement, including concerns like key person risk, dual controls, oversight, succession planning, etc.?
EG-12	What is the alignment between stakeholders and enterprise goals (when viewed through the prism of responsibility assignment)?

Sample Management Questions:

EM-05	How do we describe stakeholder responsibilities for the purposes of hiring as well as performance measurement?
EM-06	How do we measure the performance of stakeholders towards the achievement of goals?
EM-07	How do we detect and compensate for failures to adhere to assigned responsibilities?

4. The **policy framework** defines a set of principles or values that will guide how the enterprise will meet its goals. These cover both business principles (e.g. "We will never create a conflict between our distributor network and our direct sales channels.") and architectural principles (e.g. "Our policy towards acquiring new capability is to reuse before we buy, and to buy before we build.").

Sample Governance Questions:

EG-13	What is the priority to be applied to policies in case of a conflict?
EG-14	What specific stakeholder roles will be responsible for formulating and maintaining policies of various kinds?

Sample Management Questions:

EM-08	How do we measure and monitor adherence to policies?
EM-09	How do we determine if a policy is outdated or not applicable in a given situation?
EM-10	How do we intimate the responsible stakeholders of a possible need to modify policies when the situation demands?

The fundamental enterprise dependencies need to be studied with great care by executive management (aided by the CIO and the head of architecture). These dependencies and the way the enterprise decides to manage them will determine the shape of the business layer as well as all lower layers.

Business-Layer Dependency Checklists

The fundamental business-layer dependencies to be understood are illustrated below. [Fig 20]

There are three broad dependency groups that emerge at the business layer, and they are discussed below.

1. The **business footprint** is a related set of entity dependencies that acts as a traceability tool to map how the enterprise achieves its goals through every layer from the business down to technology. It describes the responsibility of each organisational unit towards achieving the vision of the enterprise, and the organisational unit's business functions that are derived from its vision statement. It also follows the business functions through to the level of processes and the logical steps (operations) that these processes coordinate. (At the lowest levels, a fully fleshed-out business-footprint diagram shows what data elements are involved in an operation and what technology components implement these functions and process/store this data. However, at the business layer, this level of detail is neither available nor necessary to consider. Work needs to be done at the data and technology layers to flesh out these aspects of the business-footprint diagram.)

The business-footprint diagram in the TOGAF model is one of the most important descriptions of how the organisation functions. It is usually not a single physical diagram but a logical one spread across multiple physical ones, and requires a multidisciplinary team across multiple business units to fully document.

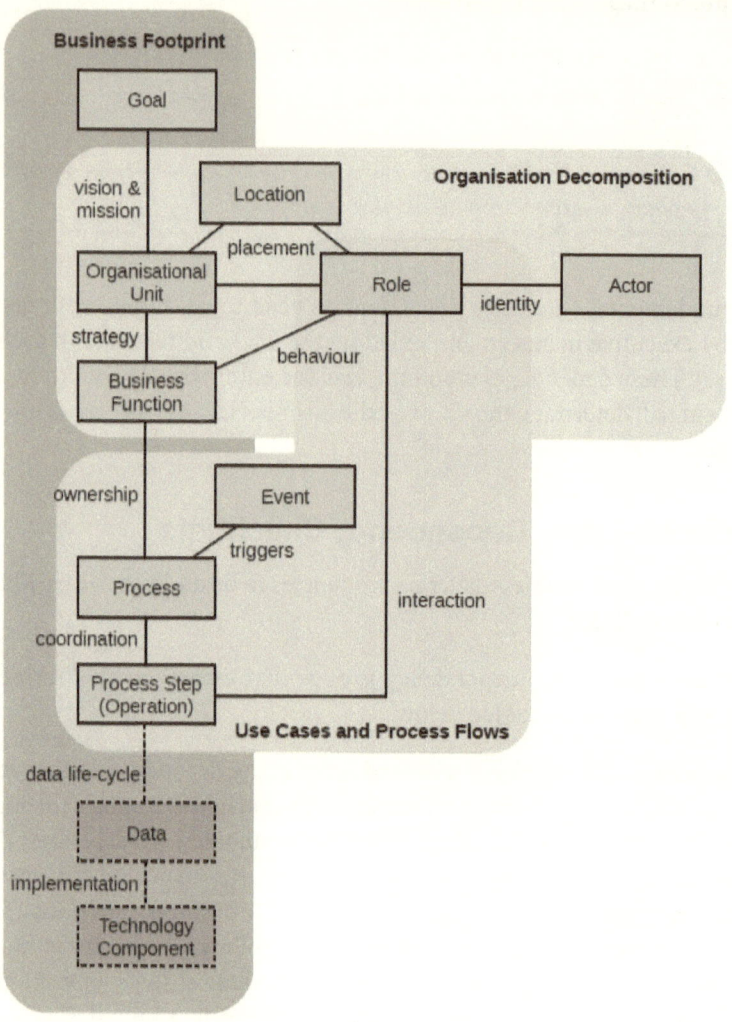

Fig. 20 – Dependencies and Dependency Groups at the Business Layer (TOGAF)

Although the creation of the business-footprint diagram is tedious and difficult, there are rich rewards to be enjoyed once it is created. This comes closest to a control panel or dashboard for the enterprise, because it is possible to drill up or down to any level to understand the implications of a change or disruption to all related systems. It is also the foundation for the application, information, and technology-layer models.

Sample Governance Questions:

BG-01	What is the extent of functional duplication at each level?
BG-02	What is the abstraction hierarchy for entities that describes how a single logical function gets specialised into multiple concrete variants? (e.g., an abstract Customer entity that has Corporate Customer and Retail Customer as its subtypes forms the basis for postulating common functions such as Registering a New Customer, which will necessarily have specialised variants for its concrete subtypes.)
BG-03	What are the factors that drive differentiation between the multiple concrete variants of a single logical function?

Sample Management Questions:

BM-01	How do we plan programs of work at every level to align our current footprint to the ideal one? (This is a high-level question that will spawn more detailed questions as one drills further down.)

2. **Organisational decomposition** shows how organisational units are distributed in various geographical locations. It decouples identity from behaviour through its definition of actors and roles, and shows how roles relate to business functions as well as to organisational units and locations.

Sample Governance Questions:

BG-04	What is the organisation structure that best reflects the functional make-up of the organisation? What level of centralisation/federation is appropriate?
BG-05	What constraints govern the placement of roles at particular locations?
BG-06	What roles required for business functions require to be within the related business unit and what roles require to be outside of it?

Sample Management Questions:

BM-02	How should resources be assigned to locations (i.e., relocation/rotation policy)?

3. **Use cases** and **process flows** describe how processes and services interact with roles as well as with events.

Sample Governance Questions:

BG-07	What are the most common event triggers and role interactions?
BG-08	What exception use cases and process flows are important?

Sample Management Questions:

BM-03	How do we best cater to high volume interactions?
BM-04	How do we deal with time-critical events?
BM-05	How do we deal with exceptions?

Application-Layer Dependency Checklists

Here's a more detailed diagram that shows a process, a product, and a service together with their related components [Fig. 21]. We also get a sneak preview into elements of the information layer because business logic and business data cannot be isolated.

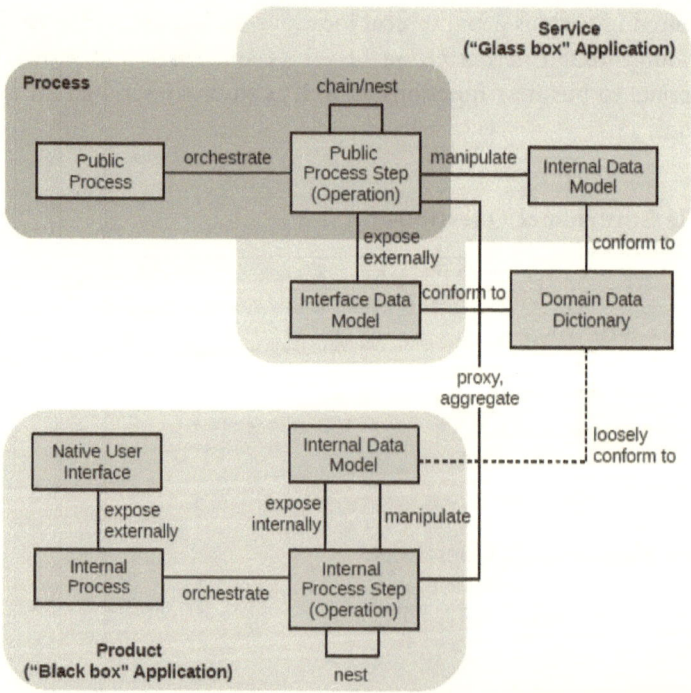

Fig. 21 – Process, Product, Service and related Entities

In all cases, there is an internal data model that is manipulated by operations. When operations form part of services, they can be accessed from external systems, and, as part of this interaction, data is exchanged between the external systems and the operations. This is the interface data model. Both the interface data model and the internal data model tend to conform to the same data dictionary, that of the domain to which the operations belong, but there is no tight relationship between them. We will see why when we study the information layer in greater detail.

In contrast, when operations form part of products (as is the case with off-the-shelf software packages), many business processes come pre-built as part of the product's functionality. The internal data model may not strictly conform to any domain data dictionary that the procuring enterprise recognises. Also, since the operations within the product may not be accessible individually from the outside, there may only be some visual means of interacting with external parties, and there is no formal interface data model to speak of. Some products may expose a subset of their operations to external systems the way services do, so this is a hybrid model between service and product.

In other words, the main difference between a product and a service is in the extent of visibility and composability of its constituent operations.

The internal data model and the interface data model, as well as their relationship to a domain-specific data dictionary, are topics that we will cover in the next section on the information layer.

With this lengthy conceptual introduction, it is time to look at the fundamental dependencies that exist at the application layer [Fig. 22].

The application-layer dependencies as derived from TOGAF are illustrated below. Note that the TOGAF model of the application layer includes physical application components, i.e. the *implementation* of business logic or what is properly the technology layer.

There are two broad dependency groups that are apparent at the application layer.

1. The **functional model** picks up the business-footprint model from the business layer and applies domain cohesion to determine which business functions belong together as logical application components (products and services). It then defines the ownership and usage relationship of these logical application components to actors/roles as well as to organi-

sational units. Logical application components may also interact and have dependencies on one another.

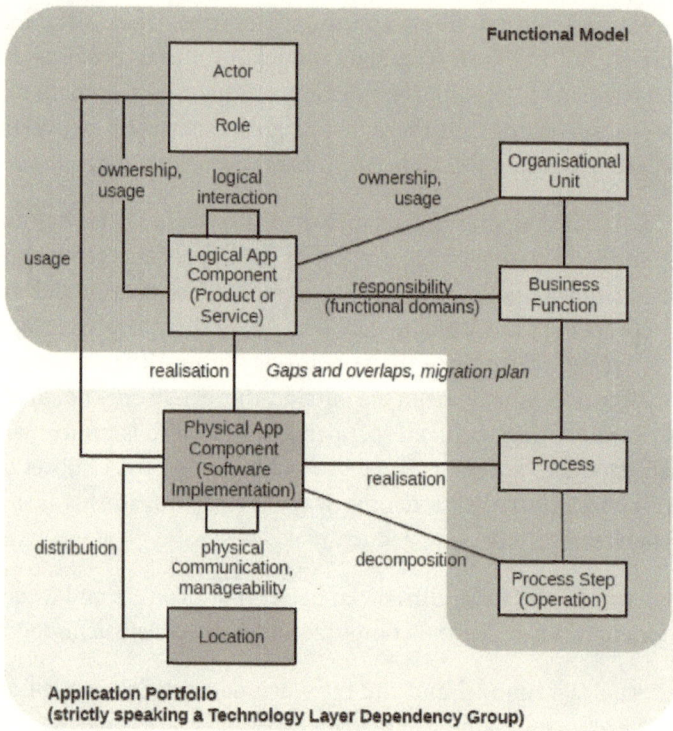

Fig. 22 – Dependencies and Dependency Groups at the Application Layer (TOGAF)

Sample Governance Questions:

AG-01	What criteria must be used to evaluate the natural cohesion of operations (i.e., responsibility for business functions)?
AG-02	(Hence) What are the appropriate functional domains into which the enterprise's process steps (operations) should be classified?
AG-03	What is the right mapping that should exist between business functions, logical applications (products/services) and implementations? What is the mapping that currently exists?
AG-04	What other dependencies govern applications (other than domain-based cohesion)?
AG-05	What interaction models are appropriate between applications? (Real-time, asynchronous, batch, etc., also invocation versus event-based mechanisms)
AG-06	What are the operations that need to be exposed (through services) to enable processes to be composed from them?
AG-07	What are the dependencies that exist between the applications we have defined? (These should be minimal, and expressible in terms of exposed operations (services) alone.)

Sample Management Questions:

AM-01	How can we ensure optimal coverage of the required business functions using our applications (products and services)? (Future state Application Layer architecture)
AM-02	How best can we procure, develop, test, deploy and maintain our products and services? (Roadmap)

2. The **application portfolio** shows the physical implementations of products and systems that exist (or should exist) in the enterprise. As mentioned, this is strictly speaking a technology-layer dependency group, but it may make logistical sense to have the same governance and management committees look at both the logical cohesion of business operations as well as their ultimate physical implementation. Physical application components are a realisation of their logical counterparts and execute processes and their constituent steps. Physical application components are distributed geographically among various locations and are used by various actors and roles.

Sample Governance Questions:

AG-08	What product implementations exist in our environment? What is missing or superfluous (gaps and overlaps)?
AG-09	What service implementations exist in our environment? What is missing or superfluous (gaps and overlaps)?
AG-10	What is our policy around new functionality – buy or build? (The answer comes from the enterprise dependency governance committee.)

Sample Management Questions:

AM-03	How do we migrate from the current implementation landscape to the target state?

We now understand that operations can be grouped in at least two different ways, i.e. by goal and by domain, to form processes and applications, respectively, and that the two domain-based groupings (product and service) pertain to encapsulated groups of operations and to externally visible operations, respectively.

Both products and services manipulate data conforming to an internal data model. Services additionally expose an external data model through its operations. The external and internal data models are loosely correlated, and a domain-specific data dictionary may be postulated to provide a common foundation to all products and service operations within a domain.

We are now ready to move down to the information layer and study the related concepts of "data on the inside" and "data on the outside".

Information-Layer Dependency Checklists

The core TOGAF-derived information-layer dependencies are illustrated below [Fig. 23], with our refinement of the data model into internal and external data entities linked to a shared data dictionary.

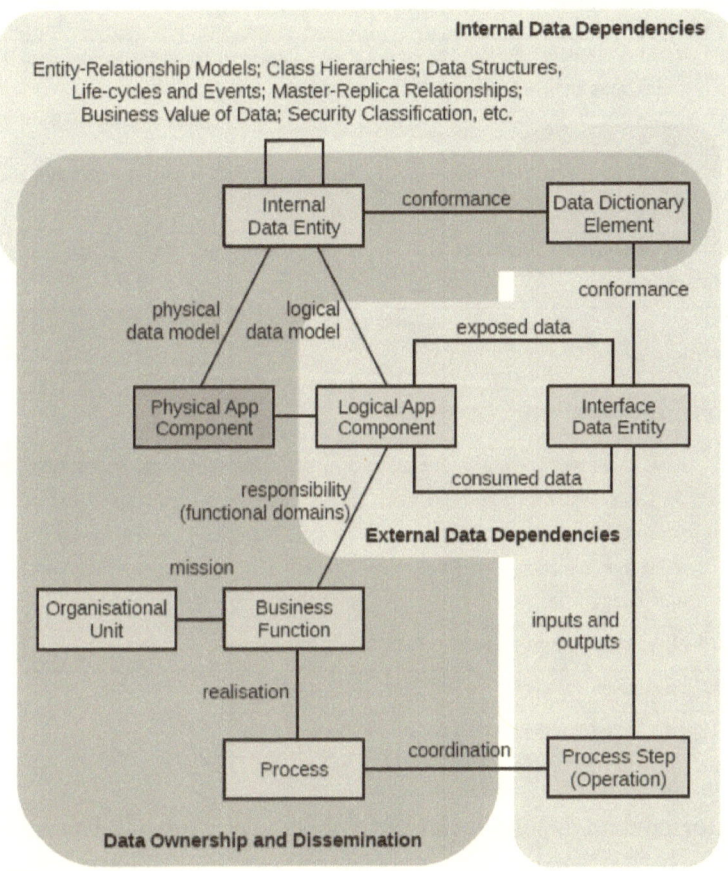

Fig. 23 – Dependencies and Dependency Groups at the Information (Data) Layer (TOGAF)

Three dependency groups can be seen at the information layer.

1. **Internal data dependencies** are perhaps less important in the larger scheme of things. The diagram lists the various types of dependencies that should be analysed.

Sample Governance Questions:

IG-01	What is the minimal data dictionary for each functional domain, as suggested by the various internal data models of applications in that domain?
IG-02	What is the life-cycle of data items? What core events impact these life-cycles?
IG-03	What data items are mastered and where? What data items are replicated and where?
IG-04	What metadata applies to data items (business value, security classification, etc.)?

Sample Management Questions:

IM-01	How do we remediate the internal data models of applications to conform to the domain's data dictionary? (In many cases, remediation is neither feasible nor necessary. It may suffice to document the logical mapping between these models along with exceptions and inconsistencies to aid in maintenance and functional enhancement.)
IM-02	How do we ensure that data is kept current and relevant?
IM-03	How do we implement Master Data Management (MDM)?
IM-04	How do we leverage metadata when managing data?

2. **External data dependencies** are more critical. Interface data entities are loosely associated with internal data entities through the application components that realise services. Interface data entities are exposed as inputs and outputs of operations.

Sample Governance Questions:

IG-05	What (minimal) data dependencies should exist between groups of functional capabilities? *(This is probably one of the most important SOA questions of all, in spite of its innocuous appearance, and therefore the one on which the Information (Data) Governance Committee should spend a disproportionate amount of time.)*
IG-06	What is the minimal data dictionary for each functional domain, as suggested by the various interface data models of applications in that domain?
IG-07	What are the appropriate data structures underlying interface data? (e.g., type hierarchies for data exposed through service interfaces)
IG-08	What is our version support policy when dealing with changes to interface data models?

Sample Management Questions:

IM-05	How do we remediate the interface data models of applications to conform to the domain's data dictionary?
IM-06	How do we communicate the interface data model of an application to others? How do we communicate changes to it?
IM-07	How do we deal with changes to the data dictionary that impact the interface data models of applications? How do we deal with changes to the interface data models of applications that necessitate changes to the data dictionary?
IM-08	How do we format data?
IM-09	How do we perform data validations (e.g., coarse-grained schema validation against base types, fine-grained validation within implementations)?

3. **Data ownership and dissemination** traces how data entities are related to organisational units and processes through business functions and application components.

Sample Governance Questions:

IG-09	What business unit and business function owns a domain's data dictionary?
IG-10	What business unit and business function is responsible for initiating and managing changes to the data dictionary?

Sample Management Questions:

IM-10	How do owners of a domain's data dictionary interact with other stakeholders?
IM-11	How are change requests communicated to the owners of a domain's data dictionary? How are changes communicated back to all stakeholders?
IM-12	How are the semantics of a domain's data dictionary explained to owners of other domains? (This is crucial when brokering or transforming messages.)

Technology-Layer Dependency Checklists

The fundamental technology-layer dependencies to be understood are illustrated below [Fig. 24].

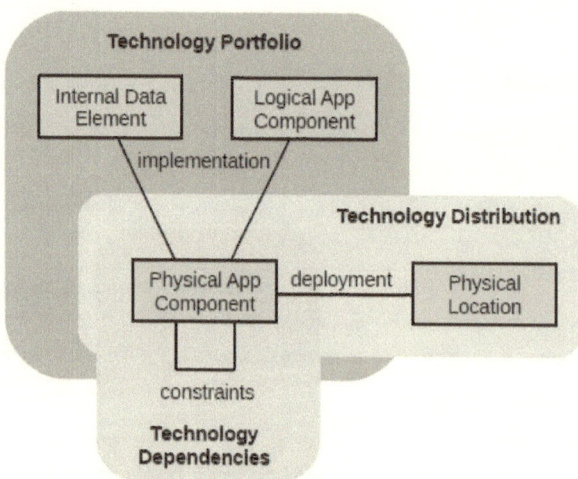

Fig. 24 – Dependencies and Dependency Groups at the Technology Layer (TOGAF)

1. The **technology portfolio** traces how logical application components such as processes, applications, and operations and logical data elements such as elements of the internal data model are ultimately implemented in technology through physical application components. This can be used for a gap analysis of target state and current state.

Sample Governance Questions:

TG-01	What data elements are co-located with applications in a way that does not permit logical separation?
TG-02	What non-functional dependencies impact the deployment of applications on physical servers? (scalability, fault-tolerance, etc.)
TG-03	What technologies are best suited to implement various kinds of business logic and data (e.g., rules engines for rules, graph databases for highly complex and arbitrary relationships, etc.)
TG-04	Who can access business logic as implemented? (Identity and Access Management)

Sample Management Questions:

TM-01	How do we implement platform capabilities (specific products and technologies)?
TM-02	How do we decommission redundant or obsolete platforms?

2. **Technology distribution** shows how various technologies are deployed at different locations.

Sample Governance Questions:

TG-05	What is the level of location-dependency of every physical application component? (Can everything be moved to the cloud?)
TG-06	What is the level of location-dependency of every element of internal data? (e.g., Legislative concerns over moving customer data offshore, etc.)
TG-07	What is the optimal number of installations of each physical application component, versus the number we actually have? (licensing considerations)

Sample Management Questions:

TM-03	How do we optimally distribute applications to where they are needed?
TM-04	How do we consolidate and migrate applications to the cloud?
TM-05	How do we track all of the technology artifacts that are deployed? (Registries, respositories, etc.)

3. **Technology dependencies** enumerate the various dependencies that exist between technology components themselves.

Sample Governance Questions:

TG-08	What dependencies should we legitimately have on platform capabilities, versus actuals? (Storage capacity, latency, bandwidth, availability, scalability, etc.)
TG-09	What market-related dependencies do technology components impose on us? (Single dominant vendor, vendor without staying power, etc.)
TG-10	What technology platforms afford us the most flexibility and choice?

Sample Management Questions:

TM-06	How do we diversify our sources while keeping the number of platforms manageably low?
TM-07	How do we protect data against physical corruption, accidental loss and data leakage?
TM-08	How do we monitor the performance and other real-time characteristics of our technology deployment? (Business Activity Monitoring, etc.)

Bringing About Desired Behaviour: Velvet Glove or Iron Hand?

Making sure we're doing the right thing (governance) and making sure we do things right (management) both pertain to bringing about desired behaviour.

In general, there are two ways to bring about desired behaviour, one obtrusive and the other unobtrusive. The unobtrusive way is often better. The fable of how the sun succeeded in getting a man to remove his coat where the wind failed and the saying "You can catch more flies with honey than with vinegar" are about this very idea.

Consider a door that must be pushed, not pulled, to open. We have often seen such doors with big "PUSH" signs on them. But we also know that lots of people unthinkingly try to pull them anyway. Wouldn't it be far better to design a door that would be physically impossible to pull? This is indeed part of the thinking behind ergonomic design. We can now see doors that have no handles but only metal plates that "call out" to an approaching person to push, not pull. These are called "affordances". With an intuitive affordance, there is no need for a sign telling people to "PUSH". It is physically impossible for a person to do anything but.

Another example is from the requirement to control speeding on the roads. There is an obtrusive way to control speeding, which is by putting up clearly visible speed-limit signs and enforcing compliance with those limits. Such enforcement may be by installing speed cameras or by conducting periodic targeted campaigns with mobile police squads equipped with radar guns.

There is however another way to control speeding that may be more effective. Clearly visible speed humps force motorists to slow down, because the price of non-compliance is a very uncomfortable ride and possibly a large repair bill. There is no need for elaborate monitoring and policing, and the expected behaviour is ensured anyway.

We could call these contrasting approaches the "iron hand" and the "velvet glove" [Fig. 25].

We are fans of the more unobtrusive velvet-glove approach because we consider iron-hand-style policing to be clunky, expensive, and error-prone. However, we recognise that the latter approach will sometimes be necessary. Our preferred approach to SOA governance and management is therefore "unobtrusive and intrinsic wherever possible; obtrusive and extrinsic wherever necessary".

However, the design of systems that are unobtrusive is orthogonal to our discussion of SOA governance and SOA management. An organisation would certainly benefit by developing velvet-glove mechanisms for governance and management, whereby everyone in the organisation is almost unconsciously shepherded into following the correct and expected behaviour, but this is an advanced idea that we will not cover further in this document.

It's certainly worth considering when an organisation designs its systems, though.

Example: Speed limits and policing versus speed humps

Enforcing desired behaviour	*Ensuring* desired behaviour
(External to design, requires active policing)	(Inherent in design, no policing required)

Fig. 25 – The Iron Hand and the Velvet Glove of speed reduction

Summary and Conclusions

//

Service-oriented architecture (SOA) should really be thought of as dependency-oriented thinking, since vitally important dependencies exist at every layer of the enterprise, and these have significant impact on an organisation's agility, cost, and risk profiles. Determining what dependencies are legitimate, and how these dependencies must be managed should therefore be the goals of SOA governance and SOA management, respectively.

The model of SOA governance and SOA management proposed in this document covers all of the above aspects. Although comprehensive, it is nowhere near as complex as current industry-recommended best practice would have us believe. In this document, all we have done is specify the core entities that exist at each layer of the enterprise, and the types of dependencies that can occur between them. It is up to the individual organisation to work out the dependencies that are appropriate to its business, and to ensure that these are the only ones that in fact exist.

The enterprise-architecture function must take the lead in driving dependency awareness throughout the organisation. Ultimately, everyone in an organisation must be sensitised to think in terms of dependencies.

Two *logical* committees are recommended to oversee both the governance and management of the enterprise through the application of SOA principles. These two logical committees may translate to a number of *physical* committees, depending on the size and complexity of the organisation. Each committee may in turn set up more specialised teams to oversee groups of related dependencies.

The sample dependency checklists in Part III can help these committees and their specialised teams to get started with their tasks. These are based on the BAIT and TOGAF models of the enterprise, although repurposed with a dependency focus to serve as a suite of tools for SOA governance and management.

We hope this comprehensive yet lightweight framework enables organisations to implement SOA governance and SOA management quickly and cost-effectively.

(Designing systems that are unobtrusive and which ensure rather than *enforce* correct behaviour is an intellectual challenge of a higher order, and enterprising organisations may want to experiment with such velvet-glove approaches.)

Contributions of This Document

///

We believe there are several tangible and immediate benefits to anyone who seriously studies this document.

Defining Terms

After more than a decade of familiarity with the following terms, it's disappointing that the industry still hasn't been able to agree on simple definitions for them. We went back to first principles to see if we could do better.

SOA: The science of analysing and managing dependencies.

Governance: Ensuring that the right things are done. (The ends, or the "what".)

Management: Ensuring that things are done right. (The means, or the "how".)

SOA Governance: Determining *what* dependencies are legitimate and *what* existing dependencies fall outside this set.

SOA Management: Dealing with *how* to remediate illegitimate dependencies, *how* to formalise legitimate ones, and *how* to prevent the recurrence of violations.

Restoring Potential

SOA has been a Cinderella languishing in a technology cellar. This paper crowns it the governing principle for the enterprise. We show how to *govern with* SOA, rather than how to *govern* SOA.

Enterprise architecture is often criticised as an ivory-tower function. This approach gives it a change agent's role that will impact an organisation's agility, cost, and risk in an immediately measurable way.

Identifying Gaps

Enterprise architecture needs a practical focus to demonstrate value. The focus on dependencies is the missing piece that this paper highlights.

We have also highlighted the need to inject professional skills from traditionally non-IT backgrounds into SOA-governance and SOA-management bodies to aid in identifying and remediating dependencies.

Simplifying Tasks

For all its ambitious scope, the approach outlined here is actually quite simple and minimal. We have provided a list of the core roles, bodies, functions, processes, and checklists that are required to implement it.

However, if all you do is *add* the processes described here on top of the ones you already use, you will end up with anything but a lightweight approach. What we are audaciously recommending here is that you *replace* your existing control systems with these processes, fleshing them out only to the extent necessary to meet your business objectives.

Doubling the Payoff

The point of this entire document is that adopting *dependency orientation* as your enterprise's primary organising principle is not only lightweight in itself, but also trims your operating model overall. It's a double benefit.

Potential Criticism of This Approach

While we are certain we have contributed something of value to the industry with this document, we don't believe it will be received without controversy. Initial reviews by peers leads us to believe there could be several angles to the opposition it is likely to provoke.

The Weight of Tradition

The first and most obvious source of resistance is from the traditionalist SOA-practitioner camp that continues to believe in SOA governance as a set of processes that bring discipline to the way SOA technology is used within an organisation.

A good rule of thumb we would suggest you use if you ever come across a book/article or an expert who hews to the traditionalist view of SOA governance is to check if they are *explicitly repudiating this document*. If they make no reference to this document or have never heard of it, we humbly suggest that our view trumps theirs, since we have taken the pains to rationally rebut the establishment view but they have not reciprocated the courtesy. Of course, if someone from this camp has specific issues with the approach in this document and is able to make a reasoned argument against it, then by all means listen to them and use your best judgement.

Making Mountains out of Molehills

The second argument against our approach would probably come from those who see our distinction between governance and management as splitting hairs. This argument may state that the functions of governance and management as defined here are both to be legitimately considered governance, so the industry is not so badly off-track after all.

Our answer is that the "what" and "how" aspects of a decision always go hand in hand, and both are important. Hence, our insistence on making a distinction between the two does not reduce the effectiveness of these functions, only the confusion between their concerns. We don't believe both can be bundled together under the label of "governance". On the contrary, it is this conflation that has stifled the real governance function.

In both these arguments, you should view this paper's approach as a revolution against the establishment line, and if you happen to come across a dissenting view, recognise the difference between a mere old-schooler and a genuine counter-revolutionary.

Drawing a long bow

A third argument is possibly that this approach overstates the case for dependency orientation as a comprehensive approach to managing a business, and that a complete overhaul of the governance and management processes of an organisation to focus on dependencies is difficult to justify and may even be counterproductive.

Our response is that all effort needs to be justified on the basis of costs and benefits. Our companion document on analysis and design details several true-life case studies that illustrate the high costs entailed by dependencies, no matter what kind of business we deal with or the level of abstraction we examine. There is serious money to be saved by eliminating dependencies, if organisations will only begin to examine themselves from this angle. Unfortunately, no major consultancy organisation, industry analyst, B-school guru, or process-tool vendor has yet latched onto dependency orientation as a buzzword, so this is not a fashionable thing to do. We flatter ourselves with the possibility that this document could just spark such a trend.

A Bridge Too Far

Finally, there is the "you can't get there from here" argument. The pain here is the wrenching change in focus that the entire organisation will have to undergo. It is a massive re-education exercise with the inevitable missteps, periods of backsliding, and moments of self-doubt that will accompany the effort. First-movers will have an additional disadvantage in that they will have no benchmark to follow and will have to summon up the will to stay the course.

But like any attempt at self-improvement, moving to dependency orientation is another instance of "no pain, no gain". Perhaps the approach can be piloted within a smaller business unit and rolled out more widely once its benefits are demonstrated.

Appendix A – SOA Governance and Management: An Issue of Definition

If you do a search on the term "ungulate", you are probably looking for what is called an *intensional* definition (according to Wikipedia, ungulates are "mammals, most of which use the tips of their toes, usually hoofed, to sustain their whole body weight while moving."). You would probably not be satisfied with a purely *extensional* definition ("ungulates are the horse, zebra, donkey, cattle/bison, rhinoceros, camel, hippopotamus, tapir, goat, pig, sheep, giraffe, okapi, moose, elk, deer, antelope, and gazelle"). The extensional definition can be used as a set of *examples* to support the intensional one, but isn't very useful on its own.

In our research into the terms "governance", "corporate governance", "IT governance", and "SOA governance", we have been surprised and disappointed to find a plethora of extensional definitions (e.g. "the set of policies, processes, controls, and metrics") rather than a simple and readily understandable intensional one (i.e. what governance actually *is*). Such extensional definitions tend to lose the reader at the very outset. Without a clear communication of what governance *is*, any list of terms carries an implicit expectation of rote learning rather than understanding.

Sometimes, extensional definitions take the form of a diagrammatic chart that lays out components in a colourful, eye-catching way (such as the ISO 38500 definition of IT governance), but even this friendlier format fails to convey what IT governance really is.

Even on the rare occasion when we stumbled upon an intensional definition, it has proven too fuzzy to be meaningful, e.g. Gartner's definition of SOA governance as "ensuring and validating that assets and artefacts within the architecture are acting as expected and maintaining a certain level of quality." Does that result in an epiphany on the part of the reader? We suspect not. In the same vein, the Burton Group defines governance as "the processes that an enterprise puts in place to ensure that things are done…in accordance with best practices, architectural principles, government regulations, laws, and other determining factors." This is an extensional definition (a list of things to consider) wrapped up inside an intensional one (a promising definition of governance as a set of process-es), with the net result that things are no clearer.

Many of the definitions of SOA governance are just plain wrong, in our opinion, and these errors stem from a fundamental misunderstanding of the scope of SOA. Does SOA governance refer to the governance of SOA assets, or is it a unique *philosophy* of governance itself? We believe it's the latter, but the industry seems to think it's the former.

In sum, all of the definitions we have come across have been unsatisfying. We have been left to wonder: what *is* SOA governance? It seemed rather arrogant to try to second-guess an entire industry, but someone had to bell the cat, hence this document.

Here, we provide simple (and intensional) definitions of both "gover-nance" and "management" that address the confusion between the two terms, with enough extensional definitions as examples to fix these con-cepts firmly in one's mind. The approach we describe is based on these fundamental definitions.

Appendix B – Lessons from Cadet Camp (or Why SOA Is Like a Snake Pit)

The author remembers how an instructor at a high-school cadet camp walked past a group of cadets pitching their tent and reminded them to dig a snake pit that would keep scorpions and small snakes from entering the tent. One of the cadets dutifully went off and dug a snake pit to one side of the tent, as the plan below illustrates.

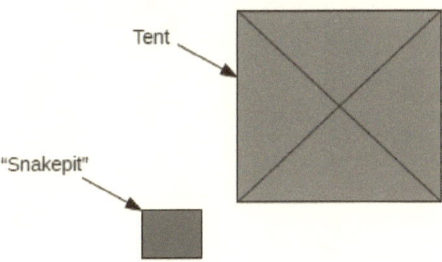

There was a fair amount of merriment when the instructor came by again and saw what had been done. The actual concept of a snake pit, as the cadets then learnt, was as illustrated below.

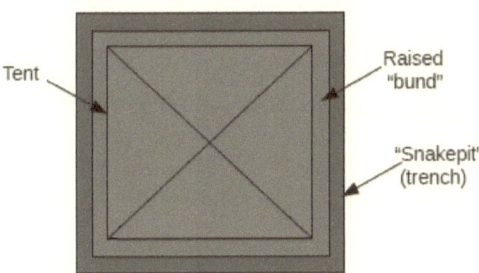

A snake pit must surround the tent entirely in order to be effective. Digging a pit to one side of the tent achieves nothing. Snakes and scorpions will not obediently fall into it.

In similar fashion, SOA is most effective when its principles are applied across the board. It's not a narrow sub-domain of IT that has to be put into its own little sandpit and managed there. It informs the way the enterprise is run, no less. It's amazing how many industry luminaries fall prey to this limiting delusion.

At the risk of belabouring the point, let us illustrate it graphically below.

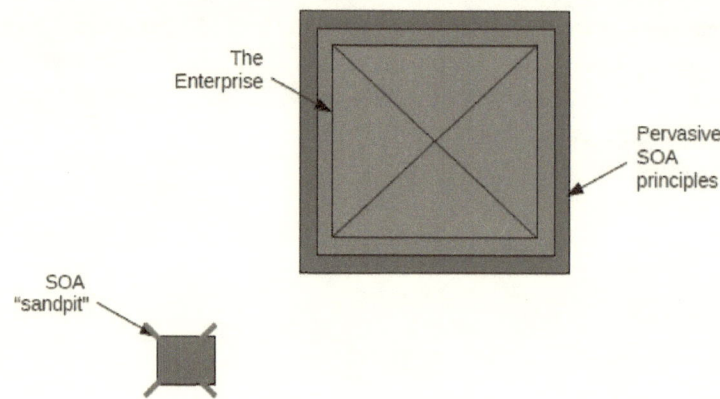

Appendix C – Core Entities and Dependencies in the TOGAF 9 Model

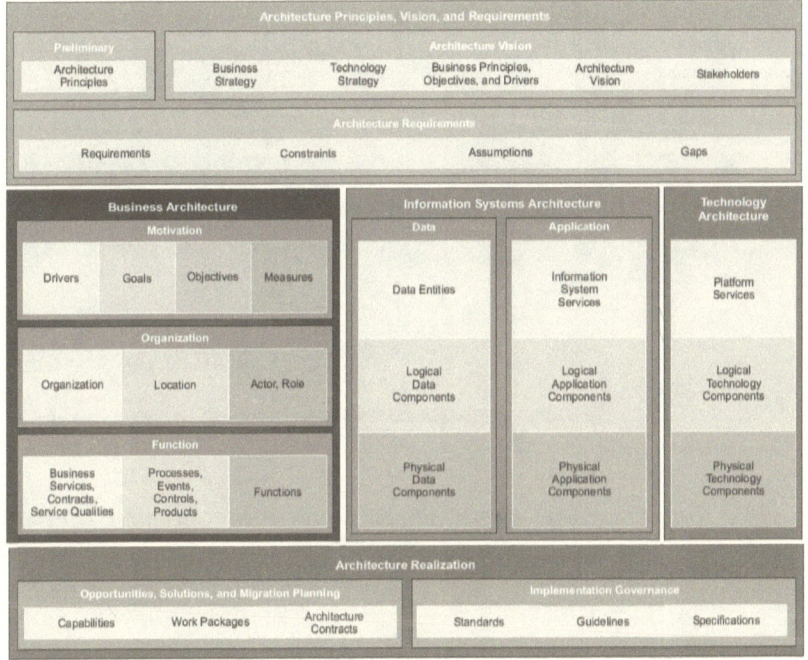

Core entities.

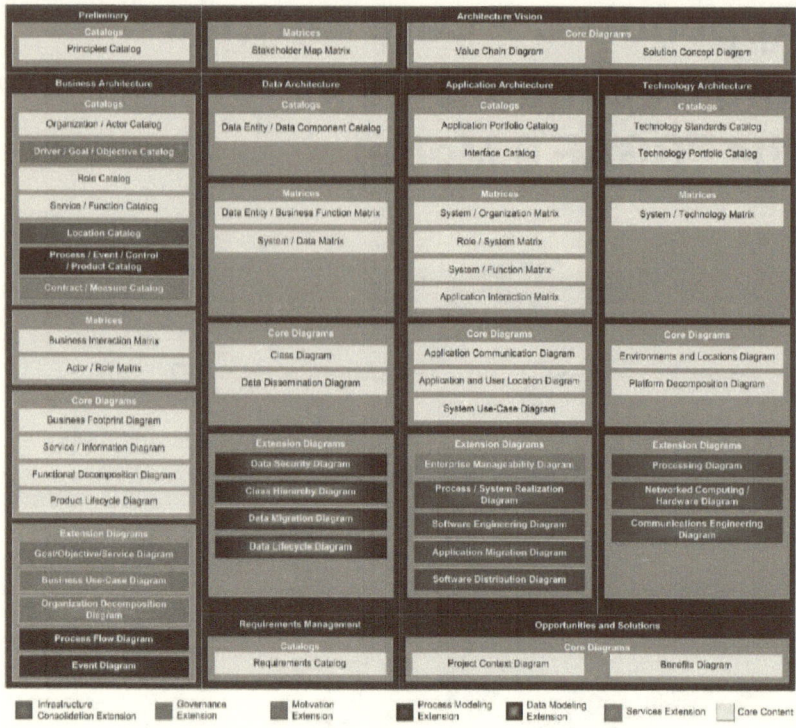

Catalogs list hierarchies of core entities. Matrices and diagrams represent two-entity and multi-entity dependencies.

Appendix D – Artefacts in the TOGAF 9 Model

//

Fundamental Enterprise Entities and Dependencies[1]

Principles Catalog

Stakeholder Map Matrix

Value-Chain Diagram

Business-Layer Dependencies

Business-Interaction Matrix (Organisations and Actors)

Actor/Role Matrix

Business-Footprint Diagram

Business-Service/Information Diagram

Functional-Decomposition Diagram

Goal/Objective/Service Diagram

Business Use-Case Diagram

Organisation-Decomposition Diagram (Actors, Roles, and Location)

Process-Flow Diagram

Event Diagram (Events and Processes)

Application-Layer Dependencies

---

1   TOGAF does not identify the driver/goal/objective catalog" as part of the preliminary or architecture-vision phases (which correspond to the fundamental enterprise level) but as part of the business-architecture phase. However, our experience with enterprise utilities/shared services tells us that goals apply at the overall enterprise level as well as at the level of business-unit silos below it, and the dichotomy is often critical. That's why we include it in our set of enterprise dependencies as well as business-layer dependencies.

System/Organisation Matrix

Role/System Matrix

Application-Interaction Matrix

System/Function Matrix

Application-Communication Diagram

Application and User-Location Diagram

System Use-Case Diagram

Enterprise-Manageability Diagram

Process/System-Realisation Diagram

Application-Migration Diagram

Software-Distribution Diagram

Software-Engineering Diagram

Information-Layer Dependencies

Data-Entity/Business-Function Matrix

Business-Service/Information Matrix

System/Data Matrix

Class Diagram

Data-Dissemination Diagram

Data Life-Cycle Diagram

Data-Security Diagram

Data-Migration Diagram

Class-Hierarchy Diagram

Technology-Layer Dependencies

System/Technology Matrix

Environments and Locations Diagram

Platform-Decomposition Diagram

Processing Diagram

Networked-Computing and Hardware Diagram

Communications-Engineering Diagram

Appendix E – References

1. Wikipedia entry on "SOA governance": http://bit.ly/HyPBBE

Blogger Dave Oliver's definition of SOA governance: http://bit.ly/H5mzY2

2. (A lone blogger gets it right where giants like IBM and the Burton Group fail. He doesn't go far enough, however, preferring to restrict the scope of SOA to just IT.)

3. IBM's definition of SOA governance, an extension of IT governance, itself an extension of corporate governance: http://ibm.co/qm46

4. An IT-specific reference model for SOA governance: http://bit.ly/H4yjKP

5. Forrester's SOA Value Assessment tool: http://prn.to/1gH4W75

6. SOA Software's technology-oriented reference model for SOA governance: http://bit.ly/HvuRYq

(Two fundamental layers: an application and messaging-services layer and an infrastructure-services layer.)

7. Burton Group on SOA and governance: http://bit.ly/HFdF6t

(Extensional definition: what is a governance program? Policies, processes, metrics, organisation.)

8. The reincarnation of SOA: http://bit.ly/9aowov

("…The old SOA had to die because it was too much focused on technology and products, while the new one, absolutely necessary for the new cloud-computing era, will be focused on architecture, principles, and practices.")

9. Resurrecting SOA: http://bit.ly/aQMCRk

("Anne Thomas Manes believes organizations need SOA more than before, but using a redefined SOA based on the SOA Manifesto, focusing on models, methodologies, and patterns, not on technology, intended to produce the desired business and technical goals.")

10. You can't buy governance: http://bit.ly/1fFW4M8

(Confusion between pages 2 and 5 – "doing the right thing" vs. "doing things right".)

IT governance:

11. ISO 38500: http://bit.ly/j3Ym4H

(Extensional definition of IT governance in the form of a chart)

12. CIO.com article on IT Governance: http://bit.ly/pz2lr1

13. Simplicable model: http://bit.ly/18XIbHh

Corporate Governance:

14. Wikipedia definition: http://bit.ly/XsnAz

15. ASX corporate governance principles: http://bit.ly/19dz1ZY

(Useful principles, partly intensional, partly extensional.)

16. SearchFinancialSecurity: http://bit.ly/e9x20x

(Extensional definition.)

17. Auditor's perspective: http://bit.ly/pkwHKh

(Extensional definition: corporate governance is the set of processes, customs, policies, laws, management practices, and institutions affecting the way an entity is controlled and managed.)

18. Data on the outside vs. data on the inside: http://bit.ly/RHj7dp

(Seminal paper by Pat Helland.)